FATHER TIME!

DAY 4

Papa & Mama Goose

FATHER TIME! – DAY 4

Papa & Mama Goose

Copyright © 2020
Enchanted Rose Publishing
P.O. Box 991
Hempstead, TX 77445

Published by Enchanted Rose Publishing
Layout by Cynthia D. Johnson @
www.diverseskillscenter.com

Written by Papa & Mama Goose

Printed in the United States of America
ISBN-13: 978-1-947799-63-9

So, who created time?

GOD created time and space.

One Day 4 of Creation, GOD divided the light and darkness into smaller components.

The light would represent the day.

Darkness would
represent the night.

No matter which part of the world we are from, seasons, years, months, weeks and days are universal.

Can you imagine what life would be like if you had to live in darkness every day?

If we lived in sunlight all day and night, our bodies would find it difficult to sustain itself without proper rest.

Once day and night were set in motion, GOD gave us seasons.

As the sun rotated around the planets, some parts of Earth were cold, warm, or hot.

Most places are a mixture of more than one climate.

Did you know that snow would never fall in a hot and arid desert?

Some parts of the world are so cold, humans cannot live there.

As you well know, our planet is divided into 24 hours.

Time is so absolute that no matter who you are or where you're from, we all have 24 hours in a day.

GOD wants us to use our time wisely.

We should live in such a way that everything we think, say, and do honors our Great GOD.

Can you remember the first time you were able to tell someone how old you were?

Do you recall your first

Birthday party?

GOD created the idea of months as well!

From what we've learned, we can clearly see that time was not a coincidence.

GOD is the Father of time.

Then, one day when JESUS returns to Earth for His Bride, the Church, time will be no more.

Those who are GOD's people will live with Him forever and ever... Hallelujah!!!

FATHER TIME – DAY 4

Written by Papa & Mama Goose

Copyright 2020

by

Mama Goose Books

Hempstead, Texas

Papa & Mama Goose Media

Through the power of their faith and instructions from GOD's HOLY SPIRIT, these humble servants of CHRIST take us back to our beginning...The Bible. Although Papa and Mama Goose have written a plethora of books, none can hold a candle to how the WORD of GOD has guided their lives. Realizing that life on Earth is temporal, Papa and Mama Goose wanted to write Books about the Bible that would provide a Biblical Foundation for young children. The goal of the books is to teach youngsters to know and fall deeply in Love with GOD.

It was during their years in college that Papa and Mama Goose found CHRIST. They were taught the Gospel and baptized into the Prairie View CHURCH of CHRIST at Prairie View A & M University in Prairie View, Texas. Papa and Mama Goose enjoy sharing the same spiritual birthday. Currently, the dynamic duo are faithful members of the Fifth Ward CHURCH of CHRIST in Houston, Texas.

Follow Me On…

 Facebook

www.facebook.com/gomamagoose

 Twitter

@GoMamaGoose

 Instagram

MamaGoose Paris
gomamagoose@gmail.com